MARS

Red Rocks and Dust

by Joyce Markovics

Consultant: Karly M. Pitman, PhD
Planetary Science Institute
Tucson, Arizona

BEARPORT PUBLISHING

New York, New York

Credits

Cover, © NASA/JPL/MSSS; TOC, © NASA/JPL–Caltech/UCLA; 4T, © Dja65/Shutterstock; 4B, © NASA; 5, © NASA/JPL/MSSS; 6–7, © Wikipedia & Nasa; 8, © NASA/JPL/MSSS; 9, © NASA; 10–11, © NASA/JPL/Cornell; 12L, © NASA/JPL–Caltech/University of Arizona; 12R, © Wikipedia/NASA; 14, © NASA/JPL/USGS; 15, © NASA/JPL/Malin Space Science Systems; 16–17, © NASA/JPL–Caltech/University of Arizona; 18, © Henrik Lehnerer/Shutterstock; 19, © NASA/Glenn Research Center; 20–21, © NASA/JPL–Caltech; 22, © Wikipedia; 23TL, © Juergen Faelchle/Shutterstock; 23TR, © Sharon Day/Shutterstock; 23BR, © Wikipedia/NASA.

Publisher: Kenn Goin
Senior Editor: Joyce Tavolacci
Creative Director: Spencer Brinker
Design: Debrah Kaiser
Photo Researcher: Michael Win

Library of Congress Cataloging-in-Publication Data

Markovics, Joyce L., author.
  Mars : red rocks and dust / by Joyce Markovics.
     pages cm. — (Out of this world)
  Includes bibliographical references and index.
  ISBN 978-1-62724-564-7 (library binding) — ISBN 1-62724-564-2 (library binding)
  1. Mars (Planet)—Juvenile literature. I. Title.
  QB641.M344 2015
  523.43—dc23
                                    2014037327

For more information, write to Bearport Publishing Company, Inc., 45 West 21st Street, Suite 3B, New York, New York 10010. Printed in the United States of America.

10 9 8 7 6 5 4 3 2 1

CONTENTS

What planet is
rocky and red?

MARS!

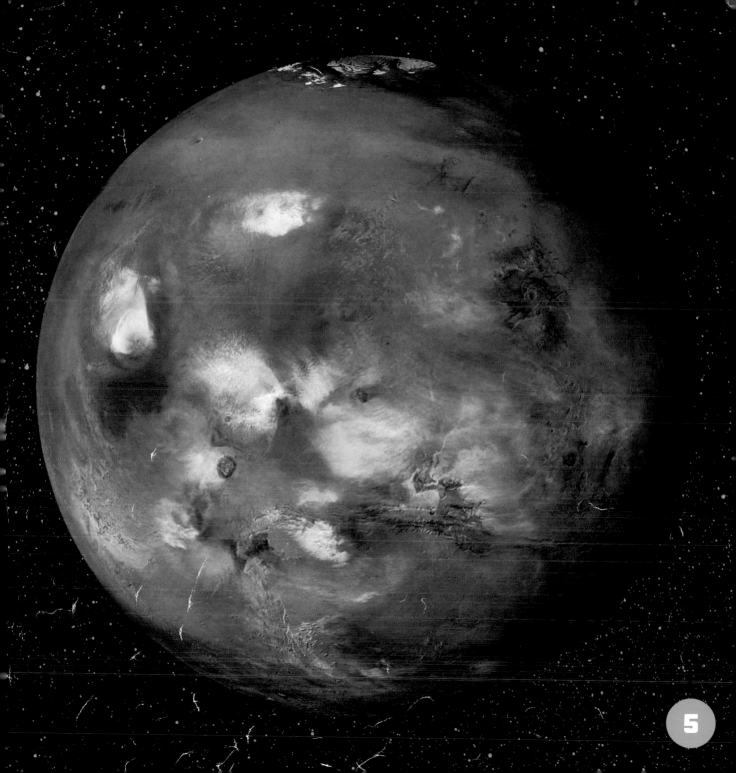

Reddish-brown rocks
and dust cover Mars.

From far away, the
planet looks red.

Mars is part of Earth's Solar System.

JUPITER

MARS

VENUS

EARTH

MERCURY

SUN

SATURN

NEPTUNE

URANUS

It's the fourth planet from the Sun.

9

How big is Mars?

Mars is half as big
as Earth.

MARS

EARTH

Mars has the largest mountain of any planet.

It's more than 15 miles (24 km) high.

MARS

A top view of Mars's largest mountain: Olympus Mons

That's three times higher than Mount Everest!

Olympus Mons

Mount Everest

Mars is very, very cold.

Some areas are covered with ice.

Ice on Mars

The temperature can drop as low as –225°F (–143°C)!

Two moons circle Mars.
They are called Deimos
(DYE-mohs) and
Phobos (FOH-buhs).

DEIMOS

PHOBOS

MARS

There is little oxygen in Mars's atmosphere.

18

Humans would need space suits to breathe there.

More than 40 unmanned spacecraft have been sent to Mars.

Some have even landed on Mars's rocky surface.

Unmanned spacecraft exploring Mars

Maybe someday people will also visit Mars!

MARS VERSUS EARTH

MARS	VERSUS	EARTH
Fourth planet from the Sun	POSITION	Third planet from the Sun
4,213 miles (6,780 km) across	SIZE	7,918 miles (12,743 km) across
About −81°F (−63°C)	AVERAGE TEMPERATURE	59°F (15°C)
Two	NUMBER OF MOONS	One

GLOSSARY

atmosphere (AT-muhss-fihr) layers of gases that surround a planet

oxygen (OK-suh-juhn) a colorless gas found in Earth's water and air, which people and animals need to breathe

Solar System (SOH-lur SISS-tuhm) the Sun and everything that circles around it, including the eight planets

unmanned spacecraft (UN-mand SPAYSS-kraft) vehicles that can travel in space and do not carry people

INDEX

READ MORE

Simon, Seymour. *Destination Mars.* New York: HarperCollins (2004).

Siy, Alexandra. *Cars on Mars: Roving the Red Planet.* Watertown, MA: Charlesbridge (2009).

LEARN MORE ONLINE

To learn more about Mars, visit
www.bearportpublishing.com/OutOfThisWorld

ABOUT THE AUTHOR

Joyce Markovics has written more than 30 books for young readers. She lives along the Hudson River in Tarrytown, New York.